GW01311196

Printed in Great Britain
by Amazon

28524358R00068